Pandemic Press Media Magazine

Christmas/Holiday Edition 2022 Volume 1, Special Issue

Inside This Issue:

1. Letter From The Editors
2. Cover Story- One on One with Char!
3. Holiday Cooking Fun w/ Mrs. Cubbage
4. The Music Spotlight w/ Sam C. Smooth
5. At the Movies
6. The TLC Podcast
7. Gospel Excellence
8. Love Notes Audio Podcast
9. Advice Column
10. The CUBB House Merch Store
11. Let's Read
12. Pandemic Press Publishing
13. Fun and Fitness
14. Share Ideas
15. Advertise with Us!
16. Writing Help
17. Thank You

Letter From the Editors

Welcome back to Pandemic Press Media Magazine- a cultural and lifestyle magazine!! Brought to you by Pandemic Press Media, LLC.- A multi- media cooperation!

We are dedicated to bringing you the best information, cover stories, feature stories, reviews, music, sports and more! We will also begin tapping into the lives of positive, industry leaders!

This edition is a SPECIAL Christmas Edition! (Our very first!) We have an AMAZING cover story and some great things for you to see! Check out this edition and enjoy!

Also, if there is something that we aren't reporting that you would like to see, please let us know!

As we see the close of 2022 drawing near, we would like to thank you for all of your support. We pray that your holiday season is filled with joy, family, friends, laughter and memories that last a lifetime. May God bless you and your family. Merry Christmas, Happy Hannakah, Happy Kwanzaa, Happy Yule to your family from ours; and a VERY Happy and Prosperous 2023!

Sincerely,

Samuel and Bobbie Cubbage

Cover Story

One On One w/ CHAR
"The Inspiration Sensation"

PPM Magazine– *Our guest today is one of the best singers in this world, who also is a friend of ours! Everyone, please welcome CHAR, "The Inspiration Sensation" to PPM Magazine! Thanks for stopping by CHAR. It's great to have you here!*

CHAR– Thank you for having me! I appreciate it. I'm so happy that you guys invited me in. So, thank you. I feel good. I feel ready.

PPM Magazine– *Tell our readers about yourself.*

CHAR– My name is Charmaine Angela affectionately called CHAR; which has become my stage name.

I was born on the exotic island of Jamaica. My family migrated to America when I was 10 years old.

I have been blessed with a powerful gift and do not take it lightly. My platform to transform lives and impact the world for the better. Charmaine, a name I say was handpicked by the divine, for I am the quintessence of its core meaning, "singer, song, delight." I am a passionate, adventurous and creative human being. Music and the arts have always given me strength to withstand the storms of life.

PPM Magazine-*Tell us about your music. How did you get started in this field?*

CHAR- My music journey started when I was quite young. One day, I was randomly called on to sing a solo in church at 6 years old- and I haven't stopped since. I knew from that point on that this is something I wanted to do forever. My brief time in NYC continued to fuel my passion for music and arts; but it was short lived when we relocated to Pittsburgh PA a few years later. All through my school years, some of my teachers became a significant part of my personal development; as well as an artist. While in high school, my English teacher encouraged me to enter a national poetry contest, after recognizing my writing ability in my homework and classroom writing assignments. The poem was called "Beneatha's Dream" based on the life of a character from the book "A Raisin in the Sun". A dream of belonging and having a place to call home. A story that struck a chord with me. And wouldn't you know it, I WON! This led to the discovery of my gift as a songwriter. At age 16, I wrote my first song, "Lift Up My Eyes/I Can Make It". It was a BIG song! GOD & I were the collaborators. The lyrics and melody came to me while walking home from school. I was feeling pretty down that day and GOD downloaded this amazing song in my spirit; and I just started singing it as though it had already been written. The musical arrangement came to me in a supernatural way. I played the keyboard by ear and arranged the music. Over three decades later, I can still sing the song effortlessly; though it's not recorded or written down. As time went on, I became very heavily active in the church as Praise & Worship leader, choir director, a part of a group; but never really thought about a solo career. I was content with the way things were.

Life had been quite challenging and I spiraled into a horrible depression. But music remained a constant in my life. GOD, once again, started breathing songs in me to resuscitate my passion and purpose. Songs were coming fast and constant- that I had to start traveling with a notebook and pen. Finally, the book filled up with songs. Then I heard GOD say, "now I have need of you. You will do a recording." Let's just say, when you live by faith anything is possible. My debut recording, "Chosen to be Blessed" was released on the independent record label, JuDavida Music Group. I toured the country opening for well known artists, was voted one of Pittsburgh's Best Gospel Performers, and was a featured artist on numerous popular tv stations. Later on, the same label produced the "Family Christmas" project; and did a LIVE recording on BET and The Inspiration Network. An opportunity to partner with a company acted as the catalyst to reside in Chicago.

There have been many significant changes in my life. Some losses... some gains. But. I'm still growing. In 2011, I decided to return to school to pursue my music degree. I have since graduated with a Fine Arts Degree and a Bachelor's of Music Degree. I have released an EP called "Suitcase & a Dream", and some singles. The COVID19 pandemic has been a time of reflection, honest living, facing truths and healing. It's been a time to reset and regroup. I am evolving and becoming my true self.

PPM: *What is your motivation?*

CHAR: My motivation is always to inspire. Music is such a powerful tool to encourage and uplift. I do not take my platform lightly. When people tell me how much my music has been a source of encouragement, I am fulfilled.

PPM: *If you could work with anyone in the world, who would it be and why?*

CHAR: If I could work with anyone in the world, it would have been Whitney Houston. Around 11 years old, I heard her music "Greatest Love of All" on the radio for the first time; and I was captivated in an instant! I was in a trance from the beginning of the song to the end. I was introduced to the music of BeBe & CeCe Winans in my late teens and again, instantly became a fan. My musical style was influenced greatly by listening to their music. Fred Hammond and Commissioned has also impacted my life tremendously.

PPM: *If someone wanted to reach out to you, how would they do it?*

CHAR: If you'd like more information, my Official website is www.CHARDreams.com.
You can email through the contact page with a performance request or any other inquiries.
Follow on IG: chardreamsmusic. And my Facebook Artist Page - https://www.facebook.com/chardreams

PPM: *Thank you for your time today, Char!*

CHAR: Thank you!

Cooking Fun with Mrs. Cubbage!!

Helloooooo, Everybody!! I'm so happy to have you here! I'm Mrs. Cubbage! I am an author, early childhood educator, wife, daughter, sister, friend, podcaster, certified life coach and entrepreneur! One thing I love doing is teaching! Teaching people. Especially young people. One thing that I really enjoy is teaching young people how to cook. Once they master that skill; along with gaining the confidence to excel in the kitchen, everything else that they try to do is easy! New episodes of my show are available Fridays at 4PM EST on The CCI Radio Show YouTube Channel! Please click, like and SUBSCRIBE to our channel! We load NEW content every week!

Since this is the SPECIAL Christmas Edition of the magazine, here is a recipe and a craft from my book, "Celebrate the Holidays with Mrs. Cubbage" that you and your family are sure to LOVE!

Roasted Turkey

Ingredients:

4 ounces of butter, melted

Garlic salt

Italian seasoning

10-15 pound turkey (But, this will work with whatever size
turley you have).

Directions:

Remove the thawed turkey from its package. Remove the neck and the bag of giblets. Toss them out, (Unless you'd like to make gravy with them later.) Lightly rinse the turkey, under water and pat the turkey dry with paper towels.

Season the outside and cavity of the turkey with garlic salt, and Italian Seasoning.

Tuck the wings of the turkey underneath the turkey, and place in a roasting pan. Use your fingers to loosen and lift the skin above the breasts (on the top of the turkey) and smooth a few tablespoons of the seasoning and butter underneath. Use some twine to tie the turkey legs together. Then drench the outside of the turkey with the rest of the butter. Place the turkey in the oven, following the directions of the size of your turkey.

Check the turkey about half way through cooking. (Unless you bought a turkey that has a red, pop-up button).

When the turkey is finished, take the turkey out of the oven, and allow time to cool. About 30-45 minutes. Slice accordingly. Enjoy!

Pinecone Ornaments

What you will need for this project:

1. **Pinecones** (any size)
2. Thread
3. Colorful pom poms
4. Hot glue gun with extra glue

Heat up your hot glue gun. Cut an 8 inch piece of thread to the top of the **pinecone**. Add a tiny bit of hot glue to hold the thread to the **pinecone**. Decorate the **pinecone** with the pom poms by adding each pom pom to a dot of the hot glue. (Be very careful doing this. You do not want to get any of the glue on your fingers.)

Allow the hot glue to dry, when you are finished adorning each **pinecone** with pom poms. When the **pinecones** are dry, you may hang the **pinecones** around the house.

****(Please unplug your hot glue gun.)****

The Music Spotlight w/ Sam C. Smooth

Hello and welcome to the Christmas/Holiday Edition of "The Music Spotlight!" As it's been said…"It's The Most Wonderful Time of the Year!" The Christmas season is upon us! For this edition of "The Music Spotlight," I will feature my Top 30 Christmas Songs (from my favorite genres.) Let's get started! Here are my top picks for the holiday!

Sam C's Top 30 Christmas Songs

1. This Christmas-Donnie Hathaway
2. Do You Hear What I Hear-Whitney Houston
3. The Christmas Song-Nat King Cole
4. Last Christmas-Wham
5. All I Want For Christmas-Mariah Carey
6. Silent Night-The Temptations
7. White Christmas-The Drifters
8. My Favorite Things-The Supremes
9. Give Love On Christmas Day-New Edition
10. Christmas In Hollis-RUN DMC
11. Santa Baby-Eartha Kitt
12. Someday At Christmas
13. Alexander O'Neal-My Gift To You
14. The O'Jays-I Can't Hardly Wait For Christmas
15. Every Valley Shall Be Exalted-Ebony Praise
16. Sweet Little Jesus Boy-Take 6
17. No Christmas Without You-John P Kee
18. Christmas Everyday-Fred Hammond
19. Now Behold The Lamb-Kirk Franklin
20. Christmas Time Is Here-Vince Guaraldi
21. The Christmas Waltz-Tony Bennett
22. Cool Yule- Louis Armstrong
23. Let It Snow, Let It Snow, Let It Snow-Dean Martin
24. Santa Claus Is Comin' To Town-Bruce Springsteen
25. Let The Jingle Bells Rock-Sweet Tee
26. Rockin Around The Christmas Tree-Brenda Lee
27. You're A Mean One, Mr Grinch-Thurl Ravenscroft
28. Carol Of The Bells-Trans Siberian Orchestra

29.   The First Noel-Andy Williams

30.   Rudolph The Red Nosed Reindeer-Gene Autry

That's it for now! Have a safe, blessed and wonderful holiday season! See you again next month with more of The Music Spotlight!

At the Movies

With Bobbie D.
(The HOLIDAY Edition!)

Hello! And Happy Holidays! I'm so happy that you are here! Today, I am going to review a POPULAR Christmas movie!

(Disclaimer: These are my opinions of the movie. If you haven't seen the movie, I will do my best to NOT ruin it for you.)

Some of the BEST movies come out around Christmas time! They always leave you with such a nostalgic feeling; feelings that you can only seem to capture at this time of year.

Today, I am going to review "A Christmas Story". This is such a sweet, little movie! It came out in 1983 and has become a cult classic! It was based on a 1966 book by Jean Shepherd called, ***"In God we trust; all others pay cash"***... with some elements from his 1971 book ***Wanda Hickey's Night of Golden Memories And Other Disasters.***

The story takes place in the 1940's, where a man, Ralph Parker is narrating a special time in his life; the Christmas where he wanted a "Red Ryder BB gun", and the shenanigans that went along with trying to get it as a gift from Santa.

For those of you who have seen it, you know what happens. But, for those who haven't, it's time that you do! I will not spoil it for you. But, I will say that the critics give it an overall 90% rating and is rated PG.

Please make sure to put this move into your Christmas movie repertoire.
(Plus…an edition to this movie franchise, "A Christmas Story Christmas" is now available on HBO Max!

Have a wonderful holiday season! And I hope to see you at the movies!

This podcast is the newest edition to The CCI Radio Show programming schedule! It's The CCI Radio Show "TLC Podcast!"
It airs every other Saturday morning at 10AM EST on our YouTube Channel, The CCI Radio Show.
Certified Life Coaches, Sam C and Bobbie D want to use this show/platform to help give you some great, useful tips regarding relationships and more.
Tune in LIVE! (If your schedule doesn't permit it, you can ALWAYS go back and watch the show afterwards.)
Please join us!

Gospel Excellence w/ Bobbie D is one of the original shows which started out on Blogtalkradio. It is your home for the 'Best Gospel Music and Praise!'' It's been on the air since 2012, and has since expanded to many other platforms, such as Anchor, Spotify, Soundcloud and more! You can catch Gospel Excellence every other Sunday on Blogtalkradio and where podcasts are available!

It's music for lovers! Join Sam C. Smooth for great slow jams and love songs! He'll take you to that place and put you in the mood! Tune in 2 Sundays a month at 10pm (EST), on www.blogtalkradio.com, soundcloud, anchor podcasts, spotify, and where podcasts are available!

TLC Advice Column

Welcome to our ADVICE COLUMN. This is a place where letters from the public will be shared; no names, or personal information will be used. And we will answer the letters to the best of our ability.

Dear Sam C. and Bobbie D.,

Hello! Thank you in advance for taking my letter. You are a great team and I hope that you can give me some advice on what to do.

I wanted to say something, especially since the holidays are about to come around. I know that this is supposed to be a time of Joy and Love. Unfortunately, I am very depressed. I have a loved one who recently passed away, and I still am mourning the loss of my grandfather. I know that I need to speak to a therapist, and I know that others are going through similar situations. But, I'm having a really hard time. The holidays are the time when we would make the MOST memories. I can still see myself walking into my grandfather's home, and seeing him sitting in his favorite easy chair, smoking one of his favorite cigars. And grandmother, baking her famous macaroni and cheese. My siblings and cousins, running around the house, looking at decorations, trying to see who can sneak into the kitchen to spy on grandmother's recipes. (My parents weren't around for us growing up.) My siblings, cousins and I are still close; but, they all have lives and families of their own. I'm unattached and I have no children. I feel very alone. What do you suggest I do?

Thank you for reaching out to us; we truly appreciate that you did. We know that the holidays can sometimes be fun and the frivolity can help to ease the difficulty and pain that you may be feeling.
We're sure that you have lots of precious memories of your loved ones; start there. Don't focus on the loss. Focus on the here and now. Your family members who have passed on would want you to do the same. Join in the spirit of the holidays with the family that is still here. TIme and life are precious; we don't know what the future holds. So, try to enjoy those who ARE here, by celebrating the memory of those who have passed. Share stories and traditions with the new members of the family, show them how those who have passed on did things. Start new traditions. And so enough, you will shake those holiday blues. Still, contact a therapist, that is a great idea. But, start trying to heal. We hope that this helps. Please write back to give us an update on your situation. Please try to become a part of the family celebrations. May GOD bless you and your journey.

If you need advice and don't know where to turn, reach out to us @ pandemicpm@gmail.com. Please include in the subject line, "TLC Advice".

The CUBB House Merch Store

Welcome to The CUBB House Merch Store! This month/holiday season, we are featuring the following deal!

Bundle Deal From
Pandemic Press Publishing!

A deal for you from Pandemic Press Publishing! Get our bundle deal: T-shirt, Mug and Notebook for bundle price of $35!

Use our contact form to order:
https://www.pandemicpresspublishing.com/contact-ppp/

When ordering, please include your name, address, email and payment method used. Payments are accepted through Paypal (Pandemic Press Publishing) and CashApp (PandemicPressMedia!)

Here is a great book to add to your collection:

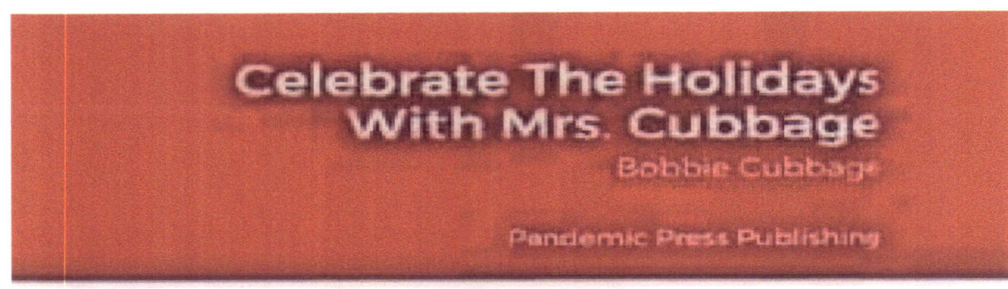

Get Your copy of "Celebrate The Holidays w/ Mrs. Cubbage" right now! For the holiday season, get it for a "Special Holiday Price" of $15!

Use our contact form to order:
https://www.pandemicpresspublishing.com/contact-ppp/

When ordering, please include your name, address, email and payment method used. Payments are accepted through Paypal (Pandemic Press Publishing) and CashApp (PandemicPressMedia!)

Per request, Mrs. Cubbage will autograph your copy for you!

Looking to get your book or other item published? Well, look no further than Pandemic Press Publishing! We are Passionate about Writing, Passionate about Creativity! We are also more than just a publishing company! Contact us today for all of your needs at pandemicpp@gmail.com or visit www.pandemicpresspublishing.com

Fun and

FITNESS

Greetings! And Happy Holidays to you!
At this time of year, everyone is gearing up for their, "New Year's Resolutions"! And the number one thing on just about everyone's list is EXERCISE!!
Everyone feels so guilty for over indulging themselves at all of the parties, dinners, family gatherings and even work celebrations! But, don't fret! You will get to your fitness goals! Just don't make a "resolution" to do so. The experts say that when you make a *resolution* to do something, you are more likely *NOT* to follow through. So, just adapt exercise into your regular daily schedule, and you will be able to reach your fitness goals in no time!

DISCLAIMER: We are not doctors or health care providers. When starting a new fitness regime, please contact your PCP or family doctor immediately.

Here are a few exercises to do at home, to help JUMPSTART your exercise routine!

1. 25 Jumping Jacks
2. 25 sit ups
3. 25 push ups (on your knees if you have to).
4. Run in place for 25 seconds.

This should help to get you on your way to a stronger, healthier body in the new year!

Anything that you would like to see in our magazine? A certain recipe? Do you know someone who would like to be interviewed? Any interesting ideas at all? Let us know and we'll do our best to make it happen!

Thank you for your support. We invite you to follow and connect with our YouTube Channel, The CCI Radio Show. Please like, click, share and subscribe. You can also listen to our secondary shows, The CCI Radio Show "Gospel Excellence w/ The Angel of the Airwaves, Bobbie D" and The CCI Radio Show "Love Notes w/ Sam C Smooth" on Blogtalkradio, Soundcloud, Spotify, Anchor Podcasts and many other social media outlets. Our newest show, The CCI Radio Show "TLC Podcast" is also available on our YouTube Channel!

Are you looking for a little writing inspiration? Do you need some ideas for your "Great American Novel? Look no further than Pandemic Press Publishing's "Writing Inspiration!" Our tips are very informative and worth a try! Lots of tips available! Visit https://www.pandemicpresspublishing.com/ppp-writing-inspiration/ right now!

We want to take this time to say "Thank You" for reading this edition of Pandemic Press Media Magazine! (As well as the Summer and Fall/Autumn 2022 editions!) All of your kind words and your continued support is very much appreciated and does not go unnoticed! We look forward to bringing you more great content in our next edition. Stay Tuned! And see you in 2023!!